My Sensations

by Gabryel Kevyn

ISBN: 0-9801432-2-5
ISBN: 978-0-9801432-2-5
The Cassie Publishing House
First Edition

Gabryel is an accomplished novelist, songwriter, poet, lyricist, videographer, and music producer. He lives in Philadelphia, Pennsylvania.

Cover Design: Gabryel Kevyn
Front Photo: Gabryel Kevyn
Back Photo: Kristine Di Grigoli (ArtChick Photography)

For more about Gabryel, including his music, please visit him at GabryelKevyn.com

I Am That I Am

Immortal I've become
A wish that I have won
I jump and scream
The happiest of dreams
Until it dawns on me
Sobering truth it be
That never ever will I taste
The Heaven that awaits.

I'm a squirrel with freewill
Up a tree I go
Mechanical ya know.
Every day it's nuts and ants
But today it seems I can't.
It seems, it seems
With my first dream
I awake from centuries free
From millennium's high tree.
Looking up to the sky
I realize I will die
And cautiously down I look...
My new soul shook,
To see, never seen before
My nakedness to the core
And I wonder
My first...
Why I'm here on Earth.

In my nakedness, I sleep
Alone in the deep
A melancholy mood
The tune of solitude
Seeks the soul anew
Quiet sound never knew

In a deep spell
Where oceans roll with thunder
I met a maiden
One with whom the earth glowed
And among such things
As I said to the trees so bare
"Where do I stand in such mist?"
And as if cavernous voices shouted
"It is true that you have found it!"
Then in the amber sky there opened,
Before my eyes alighted, the glowing night –
And as I stepped forth from among
The highest grasses, I saw, as my sight
Cleared from the dissipating haze, a
Sight of song, of beauty so fair and
True; and I knew Love.
And I knew you.

To dream an impossible dream
Means to live an impossible life.

Rain hitting water
Sparkled by sunshine

The yearning heart never stops
The yearning soul knows no bounds

What do I see

A tree I see
That will last
Longer than me

Birds I hear
So far, some
And yet more so near

A fair breeze I breathe
To help form the perfect
Cacophony

But it's me I see
Apart from all
As the desiring seed.

Tell me. How can life be led and dreams
not die?
Is not to lose a dream worse than to
live a lie?

Dreams standing alone are met only by lost,
lonely men.
Yet Time constraints where mind allows – then
and only then.

For even the brave must bow at times to all of
Nature's schemes.
Love alone, an unwilling song, will ever, ever
be seen.

I saw her sitting
Raindrops falling
Torn red leaves
Scattered, crushed.

The rain fell
Wiping her tears
Washing what pain
Delivered so quick.

I saw her sitting
I turned to go
I looked again
But she no more.

Of worlds that split
In rotation swirl,
Upon each other
The old, the new.

One side it goes,
The other then 'round,
Now past and fast
Spins to its course.

Though never touching
The pulling motion,
Never breaking
The perfect balance.

Tension and strain
And yet they're equal,
Same harmony around
A tune the same.

Neither will win
Neither will lose,
It's a whole – a one…
Spinning worlds that split.

Whose heart is it you sing of?
Is it she who just passed?
Is it another yet the same?
Who? – tell me, who?

Such light that brought a shine
To a face so commonplace;
Wondering light it is I think
For to shine so bright at night.

Oh murmured thoughts come true;
For true the heart says not
And yet once to feel such,
Another time be true.

Hatred of hate of a kind of
Thing made hard; for I
Hate the things I hate —
And hate the hatred, too.

And once I loved 'till blossoms
Loathe — 'till despise the one
Who once, more friendly now;
Whose love was mine and whole.

But again I seek to show myself
As friends tend to be; and hide
My hate of things once done
And not hate the one I love.

The flower weeps
For bright it was
Now it sinks
And petals die.

To be the cause
And being the one
Who spoke too fast
The stabbing words.

To know the soul,
The heart, the mind
That thoughts are right
And feelings just.

The world did burn
And spirit crushed
Because it's the mind
The heart does guide.

Time is longing,
Calling, seeking;
Words now balm
Amend the wound.

Holy be that man.
Poor be he.
Over there look
Another – proud.

Sad that one.
Lonely he.
The smile there...
See, it's hers.

Important that one.
Loose the other.
Hate is seen
In that one's eyes.

Another pride.
Greed is he.
Hey, wait –
Where am I?

I run home quick
To the wall there is;
I step to see the mirror'd one.

In reflecting eyes
The site is one
Seen before
As the curious one.

In ages said to be,
The little ones to touch,
To teach each so...with
A joy! – growth and love.

Their start's so small,
Might tiny I say,
Their eyes then open...to see
Crisp colours golden of life.

Her child and his, there;
A family in the park,
But none could ever so dream
Till life from joy and love.

Friends to make and soon
Then, to school to go,
With best wishes and a hope,
That cord slowly cut.

But from chest so deep,
And from my soul the whole,
I'll always be there for you...
And daughter you are to me.

Clouds grow;
Winds blow;
Seas rise;
Dark skies;

Heart sinks;
Mind thinks;
Thoughts die;
Soul cries;

Doom near;
Very clear;
Brave, strong;
No song;

Eyes snap;
Fists clasped;
Ready now;
Head bows;

All done?
The sun!
It shines;
Relief mine!

And yet Summer's so sweet
Oh be more, if not
For a Winter's bite
After an Autumn's cool.

Be not wary in days
But as a day in Spring
That sings a praise
A rejoicing song.

For times do slow
And more there seems
When again... it is...
Sweetness!
...Summertime!

Make true! Make true!
Don't sit around –
Be up at once
And stand proud.

Don't stare at this
Or shake at that;
When time is now
So now get up.

The moment's real
And well to touch
And the purpose is
So well to know.

Upon to waste –
A dreadful thought;
But let the time
Be rare as gold.

The wind blows
And strong it feels
But I stand tall
And wait its force.

It hurts and bites
But then there's hope
For storms do pass
And skies will shine.

Truth the wind
And reality the storm
The future awaits
Its hopeful light.

It's known I think
When death is near
How life is more around.

And yet there still
Seems to be that
Moment of sounding time.

Those seconds here
Forever now gone
'till forever comes again.

For days do seem
To go on and on
But soon the time will come.

When all corrupts
As here we see
Then perfection begins again.

How soft to touch
Velvet-like; and
Tall to like
A tower be.

Sleek from down
Around the grass;
And up proud,
Standing tall.

And up on top
Smooth curves around,
Softly stroking
Such petal tender.

Then wet it comes
Top and over – the
Sides, 'till moistening
All around.

Such a flower be
As when it rains
Tossing seed to
The grass below.

Hiding behind our machines
Our race remains
Centuries upon ages
Yet ourselves obscure.

Do I write ahead?
Does the past speak?
Where do ages begin?
Where do they end?

Our Time separates
Where our souls meet
Death that binds
One mind we lose.

Disrupting obstacles
Sitting in wait
The race can bind
Separate souls that roam.

Within deepest feelings
Outward it grows
A one singular,
To life's entity – Man.

What a lovely day
Today it is,
A friend is here
To spend his time.

It's been a while
Since he and I
Have sat and looked
In soft serene.

The breeze is light
The flowers bloom
The birds chirp
The sun is new.

Though the day is true
And my friend is here
Inside there nags
A hopeless pain.

I need this day
It refreshes my soul
I need this time
With friend alone.

End and beginning have come;
Birth, the death - one.
Burnings that which souls touch,
Enter upon, themselves of wonder.

Hearts – that of Love,
In dancing minds combined,
Within caged, flesh of earth;
To feel the heat of stars above.

You, the flowing blossoms of the sea,
In craft of I, found sailed forth;
Opening there in their beauty,
Waves of ocean in songs of sweetness.

Mornings, of dawn glistening,
Draws to depth my heart,
Resounds and echoes in a soul,
The drops of dew are sown.

(continued...)

As sky to horizon far,
So endless touch becomes –
A moment, a time, a breath alone
And then, to forever more.

Together, of you, of me
Is the sea – the land,
As singular sky sits above
Are then together joined below.

Time or space – distance surrounds
We in our birth (of earth);
Never outside alone you are
For I am there – for there are you.

Life's the blood of distant heartbeat,
Sings to Spirit Earth has felt,
I which now within my own,
Endless towards, of yours as one.

As sole meteors streak
If alone unseen –
No existence in sky forgotten
Not again to be.

For had not you tender been,
And there alone by me;
Such tiny lights drop forever,
In searing fire lost.

Yet upon, did you see;
And I in direction toward
From distant darkness did I fall,
Unto yours, Lights…
of Life…
…We

Eyes, of an endless depth,
To be yours, which I see;
Through the souls of wilderness
Comes the honey of taste so sweet.

Colors, shapes of hues to be
Surround my days of wonder, waiting;
Then melodies, your heart does sing...
Each moment touching mine to hold.

High, whiteness of mountain snow
Or valleys green of times forgotten;
Found you then I, in dancing dew,
Moments – forever, touched with Love.

There surely goes a woman
So neat and oh so lean
Now strutting by us so
For surely, she must be seen!

To there or here, who knows;
And if I may so say
That my eyes followed her by
Can't turn away...I try.

My heart is bare
With Winter's cold
I want it locked
And sent away.

Been through a lot
It's seen too much
I've abused the privilege;
My soul remains.

When will I listen
That to rush is wrong
And to wait not right
And what's left is hurt.

A struggle remains
It hurts again
The shell must break
For the sun to shine...

I know what it is
But it is the same
I hear the words
But what is real?

I've sorted my heart
I've reviewed my soul
The time takes well
And clear are thoughts.

But you must know
How it is with you
For I can't tell
When in silence you stay.

And then you'll talk
It's different again
Then you'll act
Not the same again.

(continued...)

You argue one way
And then the next
I sit in the middle
Waiting the end.

Let's talk it out
And mutually agree
On a simple plan that's
Not a plan at all.

But to agree in thought
Is well for the mind
But conflict remains
In my torn apart heart.

To hurt someone
Sometimes can't be avoided,
Feelings do come
And when they're deep,
It's a long time
To go away.

Life does to us, what
It wants to do,
Surely I must now know
Time's endless sting;
But then why?
And how to endure?

My heart saddens
Like a flower wilting,
It falls, bit by bit...
And with each drop, there's
A lost feeling, painfully,
Disappearing away.

With happy times
How my love abounds!
But to wait till then,
With the present storm,
The depression and pain,
Will wear on me.

My only question:
why?

Last, lost love;
Escaping thoughts.
Portraits renewed;
Mostly forgotten.

Scenes so brisk;
I saw her then.
Eyes glowing, glittering;
Darkness steps away.

Remembrance of a tear;
(though fault may be).
It fell, falling, slow;
To touch, to melt.

Leaves do die;
Seasons change.
Like moments breathed;
The wind carried away.

A lost feeling deserved
By my own means
Have I dealt this torture?
Of loss, thoughts unearthed
Growing wild, seething in need
And yet warm in intent.

How to desire what was
And in reality's eve
See the day as a Bright Star,
Above and below together –
Bright; my eyes are seen
And see through misty vales.

Tiresome without force
A Holy sense pursues my
Daily trek, holding high the
Banner, declaring time runs
Its course oblivious to a heart's
Need – oh, vilest nature!

Deeds do count as thoughts,
Ablaze in cornered lights;
The day does come to its fullness
And, as skies clear, moments
Long forgive my tears – I cling
To this time, drinking my strength.

Questions entered upon mind divided
Not clear or true I believe to be
Each moment's thought alive as one
Each day there's change as if alive.

But you remain; my thoughts consumed.

Hearts are made and brought to be
As things that burn in coldness still
The chest's deep feel knows not the reason
And decides itself what wants to be.

But you remain; my heart afire.

My loneliest thought and greatest need
Occur together so doubling the depth
Burning hate where never to fill
And left alone widens with grief.

But you remain; my foolish desire.

A breath brings life and sustains itself
To touch and feel reminds the soul
Alive to be and the will remains
Emotions defy death, and laugh in pain.

And you remain; as always to be.

What are these winds?
Won't they ever end?
While treasuring as my love
Surely being a loathed reminder,
My heart-level runs high;
My mind from corner to corner
Swimming the deep desperately,
The tide rises to consume my breath.

The time, it's sad —
Melancholy, from dismay — low,
No hope in redeeming ways
No hope without thoughts
No hope for the answer's no
And I'll burn my time,
Crying as with pain
Where sweet tenderness grows hard.

Do feelings flicker?
Or forever do they linger,
Forever reminding and touching at will;
Bringing sadder thoughts than before
Pushing moods toward oblivion
Raining wildly and falling hard
Dying in heart's failure
To be free, to finally curse.

Times should teach
But I don't listen
I care and care
'till anger rises.

The fault is mine
Though when alone
This battered heart
Would surely mend.

So, with face alight
And blinding smile
Throws down the locks
And breaks the chains.

The guard then weeps
'till then replaced —
The presence gone
All doors then close.

I looked away —
How relief is now!
A breath so deep
A sigh so clear.

(continued...)

My mind then thinks
With my heart at rest
'till next again
The day is you.

Awaiting our sleep
In dark closed hiding
Laying still
No light to glow.

Who will it be?
This year's at end
The brothers watch
And wait their turn.

Then the time does come
How green and red!
We all look up
To the magic thing.

It's flashing now
And Fate comes near
To choose of us
The one to die.

There's always one
With a slip or step —
With stems attached
Aloft we go!

(continued...)

I made it safe
Now on my perch
But oh! No wait!
My friend is gone.

He fell so swift
All attempts were made
'till next year's time
Again, we're one less…again.

I remember ago –
Do you see me?
It was you and I
With tender touch.

Am I the stranger
To the sight you see?
Do memories fade
Like cloth so old?

We could so much
And so still, we might
Move together – each;
If willing it so.

I'll around to be
And wait in cold
For you're the sun
With warmth to shine.

Don't be surprised
Or back away
It's you to me
So stay in close.

Each moment last
Is gone for good
Let's keep our time
Together, forever.

Moments glare forth
Searing space between,
Crushing hopes –
Demanding demands, that
Are fought to…
Not demand.

Times do drop
Old feelings tempered,
Pressing forth –
Trees that usually bend
Lay stiff against
A wild wind.

Deep barren cold
Growing like a seed,
Sprouting up –
To now mature,
Or care…fully…
Plucked out.

To let go
Lonely clouds alone,
Blinding truth –
Refuse now to allow,
Our forged metal
…to melt.

To pay my tribute:
Can days of life sing
Or nights cry of death?
Each time to be seen,
Each sound of breath
Compare could not
To your immortal voice;
Unending search, seething
Need, deepest heart.

Geoffrey a kinsman,
- days and times unseen;
Oh! Green Knight!
Let my soul be!
And to have your name
He who fuels the heart;
And Alexander rebuked;
For forms bind could not
The soul's highest desire.

An abbey serene across
Settling in our eyes ahead,
And each word now aglow
Tender tongue you speak;
Your shared gift expresses,
Feels, thinks, and lives;
To have without lived, then,
Your voice — I wonder
How empty I was.

Seal my tongue the Winter's frost
Seal my thoughts colder cold
For deep my time, too deep for me
How damp and cold, damp and cold.

The light soon comes, so soon, so soon
It passes me by as quickly I rise
I curse a little and wait again
How slow it goes, my soul, my soul.

Come with me for lost it feels
Come by me in dark we ride
Time to comfort, time to cry
It comes so soon, so soon by me.

The lamp is dim as things can be
The light once shone as far so bright
The dark will leave, I know it will
I wait once more, once more, once more.

For the stars passing on
And life that rolls by
As a glowing shimmer
Time moves its hand.

Little one – so lively!
Eyes and smiles
Your life begins
A heart anew.

He to hear
Your cries and sighs
Yet not to be
So troubled sound.

The end beginning
He and she
And being both,
Your heart – I listen.

I was alone,
In thought
In time...
Self caught.

She and I
Discovered two
Setting forth
A life, new.

In joy joined,
Ecstasy!
Look at us
Now we're three.

The earth grows and dies
It sings and wants
Then falls silent
In waiting cold.

But in each turn
And each new wave
There's new arousal
As moments clean.

Times pass the many
As lives committed
But seconds true
Each daily sign.

Clear in mind's eye
For when we're gone
Another will see
What I have seen.

The road winds and winds
Turns and turns
It swings and curves
Up and down.

It rises and falls
Moves and swirls
This way around
And that way, too.

What's a road?
If not a path
Does it end at all?
Or I the fool?

Tell me now
If you know for sure
How wide is it?
Will it end?

The road is life
I tell you now
Did I get through?
And did you, too?

Dreams are better friends,
With longings that leap
Or stay low in waiting,
Cursing time, sifting strength
That could be alive,
Strong it will; high in thoughts.

Few do come forward –
And of the spirit, with its
Soft-felt front, takes to
Flight, freeing shields that
Fall forlorn and forgotten
With such blissful ease.

To move, and touch;
Feelings alive! Alone
To one that alone will be;
Solitary mountains with
High fiery fountains shine,
Glowing, with heated touch.

Like a monster creeping forward,
Ever present; the will weakens.
My mind discusses and talks long,
Saying nothing; the feelings stray.
A lovely creature she is to me,
Unendless love; my heart's demise.
Knowing to forget and let live,
Lasted hope; survival's lust seeking.
Reason ends at feelings start,
Mindless end; a lost day again.

Thorns on roses scorned
As sharks steal in silence
Oh! As they often do
Coldly I'll smile, too.

With heart so long in truth
A winter's chill was warmed
How granted to those in height above
Thoughts and cares unearned.

But! The lecherous lions low!
With daggers unseen, uncovered;
Moving through dark steps below
Imbedded steel's coldness burns.

Beware! – As vipers should
The power within us stays
Like sparked burning heated coals
Fate's hand's caught with fiery hate.

Oh sir – yes, you;
Tell me true.
Of seas I smell
Of books I read;
Can things be as
They truly seem?
I know it's life
You know about;
For life is all
That's spent of you.
Your body worn
And shoulders bent;
Your mind must know -
Surely, must know.
For I have need
For me, you see;
That mind that knows
A light so bright.
But do you know
Such more than I?
Or is this life
With meanings free?
For sad you seem

(continued...)

At age so old;
With time soon gone
And life now prime.
A life I think
Is not from age;
But from our souls
Within our hearts.

A heart is life
And more the life
Greater you see
The heart must be.

The world is people
Persons the same
Earth is dust
And dust is earth.

Cruelty begins
Where hatred left off
Malice is seen
And hurts with pain.

People are cruel
Not trees or grass
Yet a flower seems
To be better loved.

People do love
And hatred cease
But the struggle is...
Few are one.

But one day
If people aren't gone
The lucky will see
That Love is Truth.

Learned men wonder
Sitting, thinking
There is no limit
To what's our being.

But life has roots
Slipping by quickly
Searching for meaning
Before it dies.

But time allows
On an Autumn day
That the truth will be
What love will say.

How Autumn brings
What wings do sing
The trees are crisp
With morning mist.

Those falling designs
With colours so fine
A cool soft breeze
Touches with ease.

I walk alone
While all is shown
My heart now light
With Fall's delights.

Could a day be any worse?
As today it seems to be
For only a few before,
Seem now, as was …then

I sit alone again,
Early, after many trials,
Tire and weary am I
To ponder, to continue

She asked me for the time
If that was what she sought
I don't know if so was
Or should I care to dare?

For before she sat beside,
With legs so smooth and full,
Intimidating me is she?
To strike a word and see?

The can almost empty
Which was so full
Now upon heap lays
Growing...cold.

He stoops so slow
To take the course
Of again to shake
A drop to take.

That might remain
Within for him
To touch to his lips
To taste, to sip...

Which so mires, his desire.

Am I seed burdened?
By such a stone
I cannot breathe?

Am I alone to die?
Never seeing the light
That shines above?

Should just I wait?
Under this stone
Till the morning comes?

My life won't end!
For I break this trap!
And sprout up,
Spring up,
Spring forward up!

My life and love stems
From the union of our minds
Can all be so quiet
From now, for all time?

We laugh and joke
For hours and hours
But at several times
It doesn't seem ours.

To sit and forget
Won't do with me
Shall we talk it out
And set it free?

And maybe long after
Awhile alone
Our love will anew
As when was sown.

To the joy of my heart
My soul will sing.
To the love of a friend
I shall speak aloud.
To the memory sacred
I remember clear
To the stars of heaven
I yearn to go!

To the life of the life
Someday O please
Someday Someday
I hope I'll be.

Is there reason
Which could be possibly
Acceptable to you
For the treatment of me?

Answers not wanted
For lies soon follow
Soon now I leave
Alone to brood.

Life is long
From day to day
How short it is
Is all I say

Bothering me
For awhile
Don't worry now you
Why don't you smile?

I need escape
In the time allowed
To leave from you
For it's foul, so foul.

How boring is quiet
So nobody cares
About things important
Even I wouldn't dare.

How I would like
To feel so free
As to ask anyone
How they feel and be.

Why can't they listen
Why don't they care
About how I feel
About how I fare.

Is life only life
With none else to share
Can all be cold
As my heart lays bare.

To ask how I feel
To ask how I fare
To hell with you all
I don't even care!

Couldn't he have been more discreet
Rather than crush and stamp my feet

Or is he the fool for us all
Who doesn't care to make a call?

That only he can and he alone
Get the information from the phone

Why must I put up with a man like him
It's a shame, a shame; a sin, a sin!

The curvature seems to be its all,
Though maybe a point it may just rise;
And has been seen, to be a pair.

Adored, beheld, and watched it is
Though physical purpose another may be;
Than the artists love or the common's need

What is this thing that so attracts
As it up and up and down so goes;
Or out and forth it seems to push?

Leave me be it seems to want
As to stand alone for all to gaze;
And then sometimes, touch;

and sometimes, touch.

I hate everything.

I hate the trees,
Birds, the oceans,
I hate the sky,
The ground and its fellows.

I hate the chair,
And that desk; the lights *too* bright
I hate all that is,
Those past; those future.

I hate you,
Him and them,
I hate hate,
And what I hate the most…

…are days like this.

And how the world turns!
Each day I would stop
Coldly putting my hand forth
Trying to stand strong;
But it comes
Passing through my desires
Laughing at my futility.

Your life's not a moment's worth
Before that sparkling hour
Then mimes into millions
Expanding past all boundaries;
Easier it is
To gain real gold
Than to bear away, your heart.

My absence not missed
To die the same
Never call, to me, woman
For I close the door to you;
I don't care if you don't care,
Since,
You desire none of me.

Love's latch,
A soft meadow;
Then aspiring,
Going forth…
We look!
Horizon's unseen;
Mindless words believed
The heart's hearth…
Touches dew.

A form,
Carried so long;
Apart but one…
And one the same,
A wandering wind
Soft it travels;
A moist mist…
Throughout,
Being them – us.

(continued…)

Falling bows,
Dark rain to plant;
Breathing souls free...
Crying as one,
Loveliness a depth
Deep with tears,
Wet with sorrow;
This hope, this one...
Patches mending form.

Death's life,
Seen in songs;
Moments eternally held...
Motionless motion;
A flower forever
With roots reaching,
Touching yours,
Together –
One.

What part of me?
Who is that there?
A man is when
All is there;
And the all be him
And him be he.

The horizon lays
Motionless and blue
Strong remaining, but
I do split...
From your different ways.

I watch from afar
As I go and do
I wait till over
Watching myself
And I all; and I together.

It'll end someday,
And a day it be
When I am me
Under one roof,
One house,
Strong,
And true.

That inner desire,
Where it hurts,
It brings me up,
And I sing…awhile;
It runs through me
A song unending,
Moments ever,
Time forgotten,
Free and wild,
Soft and clear,
But —
It's over, it's over;
My soul warm,
From its hidden grave,
Its struggling abode,
To say its peace,
To ring aloud,
And burn, the
Moment's flesh,
That worn itself;
But —
Forgotten we are,
One we must, be
Or divided, long;
And never seen
As one to be
All forgotten
You and he
Us as I,
Me.

The moments soothed were soft
All lights dimly bent
Her heart again highly leaped
Our laughter smiled brightly.

Words exchanged with grins
Eyes touching again
Our time surely short was,
Our fainted breaths so deep.

Amid the floating air
Through congenial touching skin
Our tempered heats ablaze
Searing between our eyes.

But reason was better
As knew both to be
But again not the will be strong
And feelings falling out.

Departed we are again
And not as long I hope
But time made to think
Dependent in our cope.

Lady, you are to me
Soft and smoothly silk,
Remember my mind's thoughts
Forgotten not, tender my heart.

The times, in lost times,
When little things mean so little,
When drops of lonely senses,
Touch, tap, and flow –
Are times' soft feelings we lose?
Is truly to be? And may be...
As I feel it true in solitude,
A reality ago, again, appears.

In seeing lovely senses singed
(not cooled by any forgotten, lusty spring)
And eve's electricity, forged,
Smitten, and revived again,
I, the lonely, sails worn and still,
Remark to the heavens, to a
Lovely star, "How it be?"
And yet, no answer, as lonely
Company, is still my solitude, to be.

As though trees, hanging,
With leaves sad in dew,
Secured, soiled, poisoned roots
Fastening far from life's calling.

Mornings, lonely lost;
Solitary evenings pass;
A tree, in forest alone
- in unmoving, earth-held prison.

The dreams of motion!
Of freedom; of breathless heights,
Of ocean's songs heard,
Swim in, the sea-held mind.

Then soul's spirits move
Breaking the common mold
Scorning the earth with heated passion
And bringing forth my timeless journey.

A flower, a kiss,
A friendship; in the
Light of day together,
Bring in every sense a joy,
Full to each empty void,
Beyond too, dark sky above,
Guide the stars, my searching love.

A moment, a thought,
A dream; untouchable
As each may be,
Become a night, defeated days,
Soon, quickly lost away,
Of my heart flowers you,
And fullest do my dreams come true.

A star, a quest,
A love; each at
Eternity,
Glowing bright! Eyes and days
With colours, hues to stay,
True to Love, endless, new,
As sun arises, from me to you.

As bright to me you are
And the sensations you cause,
Beware of those around
For many want, but few
Really look...for you.

You're a golden girl,
In my eyes you shine
Though in days to be...
So we won't be,
Only knowing when you're here.

When you find the time
Think of me, for
Whether I'm working
Or whether I'm not,
Thinking of you, I'll be...

Me.

I was told I flew
My body thought it so
I was told it true
And I believed it, too.
And then later awhile
As what seemed a forest
A tree in height so grew,
As trees will do.
With a bark so brown
And yet darker still
No leaves were there
Barren and new.
So did I approach
To near to see
When the sun cast down
Upon this tree
And there I saw
That there, no tree
But it was I,
So firmly fixed
So happily free.

From afar I see her
She turns and, with teary eyes,
With pale gaze never answering my question,

I still can't speak.

With her soft steps, my loving spirit waits,
Our grassy lea shortens as she approaches,
I know in tentative trembling fear...

Her love lives, elsewhere, still...

If ever a moment
Could be forever
So could a breath
Mean so much.

I slip into this dream
Never awakening
As we journey together
As one,

None can touch.

Subjugation
Masturbation
Congregation
Realization
Fornication
Situation
Regulation
Actualization
Combination
Desecration
Motivation
Altercation
Fabrication
Copulation
Salivation
Abomination
Damnation
Salutation
Libations
Sensation
Creation
Revelation
Hu
Man
Con
Di
Tion

www.ingramcontent.com/pod-product-compliance
Lightning Source LLC
LaVergne TN
LVHW041205080426
835508LV00008B/811